10 MINUTE

MOMENTS

SERIES

The RED STUFF

EXPLORING THE WORDS
OF JESUS TEN MINUTES
AT A TIME

by Scott Rubin

 simply for students

10-Minute Moments: The Red Stuff
Exploring the Words of Jesus Ten Minutes At a Time

Credits
Author: Scott Rubin
Executive Developer: Nadim Najm
Chief Creative Officer: Joani Schultz
Assistant Editor: Rob Cunningham
Cover Art Director: Riley Hall
Designer: Veronica Lucas
Production Manager: DeAnne Lear

Unless otherwise indicated, all Scripture quotations are taken from
the Holy Bible, New Living Translation, copyright © 1996, 2004, 2007.
Used by permission of Tyndale House Publishers, Inc., Carol Stream,
Illinois 60188. All rights reserved.

10   17 16 15 14
Printed in the United States of America.

INTRODUCTION

Hey!

What you hold in your hands is some powerful stuff. And I'm not saying that because I wrote it. I say it because this daily devotional is packed full of the words of the one and only, real-life original, master of the universe, Jesus. And he spoke words that heal, words that challenge, words that convict, and words that fill us with the knowledge and wisdom of God.

See? Powerful stuff! Like eating jalapeños coated in hot sauce and dipped in lava.

The whole point of this book is very simple: Give God 10 minutes a day for one month, and let him into your life. Let him speak to your heart. And let him show you all the cool stuff he has in store for you.

Too big a promise? No way! God's good for it. After all, he wants you to experience life to the fullest, one day at a time.

Just 10 minutes a day. 10 minutes! (Some of you spend more than 10 minutes trying to find where you put your other flip-flop. You might spend more than 10 minutes pounding on the bathroom door trying to get your sister to let you in. Or maybe you spend more than 10 minutes flipping channels and watching basically nothing on TV. But you could also spend 10 minutes with God—and see what he does with it.)

These 10-minute moments are going to invite you into the very words that Jesus spoke when he was on the planet. These words are so important that lots of Bibles printed them in red, so that we wouldn't miss them. And my good friend Leah Gleason, who's super smart and knows a TON about the Bible, worked really hard to make sure that each of these 10-minute moments would be worth your time and help you understand Jesus a little bit better. I think you're going to be amazed with what God can do when you focus on his words for even 10 minutes.

So dig in!

Scott

Scott Rubin

The first written record of Jesus' words ("The Red Stuff!") is when he was 12 years old. How cool is that?! Jesus really did experience life as a teenager.

And—interestingly—this first episode shows Jesus seeing things differently than his parents did. (I bet that's happened to you at least once, huh?) But even though Jesus was a human 12-year-old in a tense moment with his parents, there are strong clues that this Jesus was no "regular kid."

2 MINUTES

Read the passage below. Circle or underline any words/phrases/ verses that you feel are important to remember.

Luke 2:41-52 (NLT)

41 Every year Jesus' parents went to Jerusalem for the Passover festival. 42 When Jesus was twelve years old, they attended the festival as usual. 43 After the celebration was over, they started home to Nazareth, but Jesus stayed behind in Jerusalem. His parents didn't miss him at first, 44 because they assumed he was among the other travelers. But when he didn't show up that evening, they started looking for him among their relatives and friends.

45 When they couldn't find him, they went back to Jerusalem to search for him there. 46 Three days later they finally discovered him in the Temple, sitting among the religious teachers, listening to them and asking questions. 47 All who heard him were amazed at his understanding and his answers. 48 His parents didn't know what to

*think. "Son," his mother said to him, "why have you done this to us?
Your father and I have been frantic, searching for you everywhere."*

*⁴⁹ "But why did you need to search?" he asked. "Didn't you know
that I must be in my Father's house?" ⁵⁰ But they didn't understand
what he meant.*

*⁵¹ Then he returned to Nazareth with them and was obedient to
them. And his mother stored all these things in her heart.*

*⁵² Jesus grew in wisdom and in stature and in favor with God and all
the people.*

Think about the following questions and how they might apply to
your life.
- After reading Luke 2:41-52, what are some of the clues that
  Jesus was no "regular kid"?
- Verse 46 says Joseph and Mary found Jesus sitting among the
  religious teachers in the temple. The teachers were amazed at
  his understanding and his answers. What do you think Jesus
  might have been talking about with them?
- Can you imagine being in Jesus' shoes, sitting among a bunch
  of church leaders who are amazed at your understanding and
  answers about the Bible? How do you think you would feel?
- When Jesus' parents confronted him about where he'd been,
  Jesus replied, "Why were you searching for me? Didn't you
  know I had to be in my Father's house?" What do you think
  Jesus meant? What makes you think that?
- Verse 51 says Mary "stored" these thoughts in her heart,
  meaning that she kept them in her memory. What do you think
  Mary specifically "stored" in her heart about Jesus? Why do you
  think the verse mentions that?

3 MINUTES

Hanging out with God
- What is something about Jesus that you have stored or kept close to your heart?
- Is it something he has done or something he has said in Scripture that has been really meaningful to you?
- Spend a minute reflecting on a memory you have about Jesus, and then share it with God in prayer.

THOUGHTS

This space is here for you to jot down some thoughts, write out a prayer, draw a picture, or do whatever you want to help you remember your 10-minute moment.

NICODEMUS REBORN!

So there was this guy named Nicodemus—he was kind of a big-deal religious leader. The religious leaders were mostly concerned with making sure everybody followed all the rules they'd made. But Nicodemus heard about Jesus, and he wanted to know more about him. He sneaked out to meet Jesus at night and ask him some questions. Look for one of the most famous (and important!) verses in the Bible, toward the end of this section.

2 MINUTES

Read the passage below. Circle or underline any words/phrases/verses that you feel are important to remember.

John 3:1-17 (NLT)
¹ There was a man named Nicodemus, a Jewish religious leader who was a Pharisee. ² After dark one evening, he came to speak with Jesus. "Rabbi," he said, "we all know that God has sent you to teach us. Your miraculous signs are evidence that God is with you."

³ Jesus replied, "I tell you the truth, unless you are born again, you cannot see the Kingdom of God."

⁴ "What do you mean?" exclaimed Nicodemus. "How can an old man go back into his mother's womb and be born again?"

⁵ Jesus replied, "I assure you, no one can enter the Kingdom of God without being born of water and the Spirit. ⁶ Humans can reproduce only human life, but the Holy Spirit gives birth to spiritual life. ⁷ So don't be surprised when I say, 'You must be born again.' ⁸ The wind blows wherever it wants. Just as you can hear the wind but can't tell where it comes from or where it is going, so you can't explain how people are born of the Spirit."

⁹ "How are these things possible?" Nicodemus asked.

¹⁰ Jesus replied, "You are a respected Jewish teacher, and yet you don't understand these things? ¹¹ I assure you, we tell you what we know and have seen, and yet you won't believe our testimony. ¹² But if you don't believe me when I tell you about earthly things, how can you possibly believe if I tell you about heavenly things? ¹³ No one has ever gone to heaven and returned. But the Son of Man has come down from heaven. ¹⁴ And as Moses lifted up the bronze snake on a pole in the wilderness, so the Son of Man must be lifted up, ¹⁵ so that everyone who believes in him will have eternal life.

¹⁶ "For God loved the world so much that he gave his one and only Son, so that everyone who believes in him will not perish but have eternal life. ¹⁷ God sent his Son into the world not to judge the world, but to save the world through him."

Think about the following questions and how they might apply to your life.

- Verse 1 reveals that Nicodemus is a Pharisee. What do you think a Pharisee is?
- Why do you think Nicodemus sneaked out at night to meet Jesus? Do you think he was worried about being caught? Why or why not?
- In verse 3, Jesus tells Nicodemus that he must be born again. How does Nicodemus respond? Why do you think he responded that way?
- If someone asked you, how would you describe what it means to be born again?
- Did you catch one of the most famous verses in the Bible? What is it? Do you agree this verse is important? Why or why not? (Hint: It's verse 16!)

3 MINUTES

Hanging out with God

- Is there something that you've always wanted to ask Jesus? Maybe it's something you've been afraid to say out loud or in front of others because of what they might say. Take some time and write/journal a letter to God and ask him anything that might be on your mind.

THOUGHTS

This space is here for you to jot down some thoughts, write out a prayer, draw a picture, or do whatever you want to help you remember your 10-minute moment.

Day 3 — JESUS CALLS MATTHEW

Matthew (also called Levi) was a tax collector, not a job that attracted many friends—kind of like ticketing parked cars or towing them away. Even though tax collectors were looked down upon in those days, Matthew was one of the first people Jesus invited to follow him, and the religious leaders had a real problem with that! They thought that Jesus hung out with "sinful people" way too much. But in this Red Stuff, Jesus made it clear why he came. And it wasn't to only hang out with "church people."

Read the passage below. Circle or underline any words/phrases/ verses that you feel are important to remember.

Mark 2:13-17 (NIV)
13 Once again Jesus went out beside the lake. A large crowd came to him, and he began to teach them. 14 As he walked along, he saw Levi son of Alphaeus sitting at the tax collector's booth. "Follow me," Jesus told him, and Levi got up and followed him.

15 While Jesus was having dinner at Levi's house, many tax collectors and "sinners" were eating with him and his disciples, for there were many who followed him. 16 When the teachers of the law who were Pharisees saw him eating with the "sinners" and tax collectors, they asked his disciples: "Why does he eat with tax collectors and 'sinners'?"

17 On hearing this, Jesus said to them, "It is not the healthy who need a doctor, but the sick. I have not come to call the righteous, but sinners."

5 MINUTES

Think about the following questions and how they might apply to your life.

- Matthew is one of the first people Jesus called to follow him. Why do you think Jesus might have chosen him to be one of the first disciples?
- What was Matthew's response to Jesus? If you were Matthew, what do you think you would have done?
- Why do you think the religious leaders had such a problem with Jesus eating with tax collectors and "sinners"? Why was this such a big deal?
- If asked to explain what Jesus meant in his response to the religious leaders (verse 17), what would you say?
- Think about where you sit for lunch at school; who are the people you sit with? Are they all church people? Or does anyone at your lunch table even know that you follow Jesus?

3 MINUTES

Hanging out with God

- Have you ever thought that God might have placed you at the exact lunch table, classroom, sports team, or extracurricular activity for a reason? Maybe it's not just an accident! Pray and ask God if there's anyone he wants you to befriend.

THOUGHTS

This space is here for you to jot down some thoughts, write out a prayer, draw a picture, or do whatever you want to help you remember your 10-minute moment.

Day 4

SALT AND LIGHT

In The Red Stuff, you'll find that Jesus loves to use everyday objects to make a point. He compares his followers to salt (used for flavoring and for preserving stuff) and light (you know what light is for, right?). Jesus believes his followers should have a positive effect on those around them. It's what we were made to do! When you're reading this one, remember that he's not talking about "actual" salt and light, but about how you and I are designed to impact those around us!

2 MINUTES

Read the passage below. Circle or underline any words/phrases/verses that you feel are important to remember.

Matthew 5:13-16 (NLT)

13 "You are the salt of the earth. But what good is salt if it has lost its flavor? Can you make it salty again? It will be thrown out and trampled underfoot as worthless.

14 "You are the light of the world—like a city on a hilltop that cannot be hidden. 15 No one lights a lamp and then puts it under a basket. Instead, a lamp is placed on a stand, where it gives light to everyone in the house. 16 In the same way, let your good deeds shine out for all to see, so that everyone will praise your heavenly Father."

5 MINUTES

Think about the following questions and how they might apply to your life.

- In verse 13, Jesus compares his followers to salt. In your own words explain why you think he picked salt for his comparison. In what ways are his followers like salt?
- Jesus talks about the danger of salt losing its flavor. In the same way, we can sometimes lose our "zest" for living for God. What kind of things can you do to maintain your "saltiness"?
- In verse 14, Jesus compares his followers to light. What do you think Jesus meant by that?
- In verse 15, Jesus says that people don't light a lamp and put it under a basket. Describe a time or situation when it was hard for you to shine your light. Why was it hard?
- Can you recall a time when you "shined your light" and it made a difference? Where were you and what happened?
- Do you think it's important to be salt and light? Is it easy? Why or why not?

3 MINUTES

Hanging out with God

- Jesus loved using everyday objects to make a point, like comparing his followers to salt and light. Invite God with you and take a walk around your house (seriously, do it!) and see if you can find any other objects that can be compared to being a follower of Jesus.

10

THOUGHTS

This space is here for you to jot down some thoughts, write out a prayer, draw a picture, or do whatever you want to help you remember your 10-minute moment.

I SWEAR TO...

Do you have trustworthy friends? Like, when they tell you something is true, they don't have to "triple-secret-super-pinky-promise" in order for you to believe them? Usually when someone tells us something that seems almost unbelievable, the first thing we do is consider how truthful this friend has been in the past. "Does this person have a history of telling me crazy stuff that turns out to be false?" And when Jesus talks in this passage about "vows," he means when someone says, "I swear to (whatever)." That's often what people think they need to say, in order to get people to believe them. In this Red Stuff, Jesus tells of a better way.

Read the passage below. Circle or underline any words/phrases/ verses that you feel are important to remember.

Matthew 5:33-37 (NLT)
33 "You have also heard that our ancestors were told, 'You must not break your vows; you must carry out the vows you make to the Lord.' 34 But I say, do not make any vows! Do not say, 'By heaven!' because heaven is God's throne. 35 And do not say, 'By the earth!' because the earth is his footstool. And do not say, 'By Jerusalem!' for Jerusalem is the city of the great King. 36 Do not even say, 'By my head!' for you can't turn one hair white or black. 37 Just say a simple, 'Yes, I will,' or 'No, I won't.' Anything beyond this is from the evil one.

5 MINUTES

Think about the following questions and how they might apply to your life.

- What does it mean to be trustworthy? Do you have friends who are trustworthy—who always keep their promises? If so, who?
- If someone were to ask your friends if you are trustworthy, what do you think they would say? Why?
- Have any of your friends broken your trust? Maybe they lied or revealed important information about you that you asked not be shared. How did it make you feel?
- How does Jesus tell us to live in verse 37? Do you think this is easy or difficult to do? Do you think it's important to live out? Why or why not?
- How do you do with keeping promises to people—following through on your "Yes, I will" or "No, I won't"? What can you do to grow in this area?

3 MINUTES

Hanging out with God

- When we know and love God deeply, we can't help but want to follow his commands. And we can know God more by hanging out with him! One way we can hang out with God is listening to worship music. Do you have a favorite worship song? Why is it one of your favorites? What does it tell you about God?
- Use your 3 minutes by finding a comfortable place and imagine God sitting with you as you listen to one of your favorite worship songs.

THOUGHTS

This space is here for you to jot down some thoughts, write out a prayer, draw a picture, or do whatever you want to help you remember your 10-minute moment.

Day 6

LOVE YOUR... ENEMIES?

Friends are great, but none of them are perfect, right? Sometimes it can be really tough to show kindness to our friends and family. But in The Red Stuff, Jesus (not surprisingly, by now) is saying something that almost sounds crazy. He says that God wants you to do more than just care about the people who already love you; God wants you to intentionally do cool stuff for people who don't like you! This is one of Jesus' teachings that might make you think to yourself, "Can he really be serious?" But if you take a few minutes to really think about what Jesus is saying, you can see that this is the kind of mind-blowing teaching that really could change the world!

2 MINUTES

Read the passage below. Circle or underline any words/phrases/verses that you feel are important to remember.

Luke 6:27-36 (NLT) (You can also read Matthew's version of this story in Matthew 5:43-48.)

[27] *"But to you who are willing to listen, I say, love your enemies! Do good to those who hate you.* [28] *Bless those who curse you. Pray for those who hurt you.* [29] *If someone slaps you on one cheek, offer the other cheek also. If someone demands your coat, offer your shirt also.* [30] *Give to anyone who asks; and when things are taken away from you, don't try to get them back.* [31] *Do to others as you would like them to do to you.*

[32] *"If you love only those who love you, why should you get credit for that? Even sinners love those who love them!* [33] *And if you do good*

only to those who do good to you, why should you get credit? Even sinners do that much! ³⁴ *And if you lend money only to those who can repay you, why should you get credit? Even sinners will lend to other sinners for a full return.*

³⁵ *"Love your enemies! Do good to them. Lend to them without expecting to be repaid. Then your reward from heaven will be very great, and you will truly be acting as children of the Most High, for he is kind to those who are unthankful and wicked.* ³⁶ *You must be compassionate, just as your Father is compassionate.*

Think about the following questions and how they might apply to your life.

Grab a Bible and read Matthew 5:43-48. This is the account from Matthew (same guy as "Levi" from Day 3) of what Jesus said about loving your enemies.

- What are the similarities and differences between these passages? What can you learn from reading the passages from both Luke and Matthew?
- Re-read Luke 6:27-36. Do you think these verses would be hard for you to live out? Why or why not?
- When you read these verses, does someone come to mind who might be hard for you to love or treat this way? Why is it hard for you to love that person?
- What do you think might get in the way of you loving your enemies?
- What do you think might happen if we all started to love our enemies? How might it change things in our world?

Hanging out with God
- The cool thing about Jesus is that he didn't just teach this stuff; he actually lived it out! Even while he was dying (dying!) on the cross, Jesus prayed for those who mocked him.

- Take a few moments and think of someone who might be hard for you to love. Invite God into your thoughts and tell him about this person. If you feel like you are ready to take the next step, ask God to help you see this person the way that he sees this person, and to show you how to take one step toward caring for this person.

This space is here for you to jot down some thoughts, write out a prayer, draw a picture, or do whatever you want to help you remember your 10-minute moment.

Day 7

READING GOD'S MIND

Jesus loved to tell stories. He especially loved telling stories that made people think about things in new ways. In today's episode of The Red Stuff, Jesus makes a comparison between asking a friend for something and asking God for something.

2 MINUTES

Read the passage below. Circle or underline any words/phrases/verses that you feel are important to remember.

Luke 11:5-13 (NLT) (You can also read Matthew's version of this story in Matthew 7:7-11.)

5 Then, teaching them more about prayer, he used this story: "Suppose you went to a friend's house at midnight, wanting to borrow three loaves of bread. You say to him, 6 'A friend of mine has just arrived for a visit, and I have nothing for him to eat.' 7 And suppose he calls out from his bedroom, 'Don't bother me. The door is locked for the night, and my family and I are all in bed. I can't help you.' 8 But I tell you this—though he won't do it for friendship's sake, if you keep knocking long enough, he will get up and give you whatever you need because of your shameless persistence.

9 "And so I tell you, keep on asking, and you will receive what you ask for. Keep on seeking, and you will find. Keep on knocking, and the door will be opened to you. 10 For everyone who asks, receives. Everyone who seeks, finds. And to everyone who knocks, the door will be opened.

[11] *"You fathers—if your children ask for a fish, do you give them a snake instead? [12] Or if they ask for an egg, do you give them a scorpion? Of course not! [13] So if you sinful people know how to give good gifts to your children, how much more will your heavenly Father give the Holy Spirit to those who ask him."*

Think about the following questions and how they might apply to your life.

- If you were honest about your prayer life (talking with God), how would you describe it?
  a. I hang out with God every day.
  b. I catch up with God once or twice a week.
  c. I check in with God when I go to church.
  d. I'm busy and don't get a chance to talk with God much.
- Rank the importance of prayer on a scale of 1-10. [1 = not important; 10 = incredibly important]
- Explain your ranking.
- Do you ever feel like God isn't listening to you when you pray? If so, describe a time you felt this way.
- Re-read the passage from Luke 11 again. What can you learn about God and his character from this passage?
- What can you learn about God in the way he responds to prayer?

Hanging out with God
- One of the coolest ways to see how God answers prayers is through a prayer journal. It's simple: Grab a blank notebook and start writing your thoughts and prayers to God. After you start filling it up, you can look back and re-read the prayers that you have wrote and see how God has answered them (with a "YES" or "NO" or "WAIT").

- Take time today to write out your thoughts to God. You can share your day with him, thank him for who he is or things that have happened to you, ask him for advice, or pray for other people who might be going through a rough time. You can tell, ask, or share anything with God!

This space is here for you to jot down some thoughts, write out a prayer, draw a picture, or do whatever you want to help you remember your 10-minute moment.

Day 8

NEED A BREAK?

This is a short section of Red Stuff, with a whole lot of power! Some people think following Jesus requires a long set of rules to follow and an exhausting to-do list to complete. But instead of loading us up with stuff that will weigh us down, Jesus says that living his way will actually lighten our load. Christianity is not about filling your backpack with heavy bricks that will make life harder, but about pulling bricks out of your backpack, to live more freely!

Read the passage below. Circle or underline any words/phrases/ verses that you feel are important to remember.

Matthew 11:28-30 (NLT)
28 Then Jesus said, "Come to me, all of you who are weary and carry heavy burdens, and I will give you rest. 29 Take my yoke upon you. Let me teach you, because I am humble and gentle at heart, and you will find rest for your souls. 30 For my yoke is easy to bear, and the burden I give you is light."

Think about the following questions and how they might apply to your life.
- Describe a time you felt overwhelmed or "heavy" from all that life threw at you. What do you usually do when you feel this way?

- In verse 28, what is Jesus' first instruction when you are weary and carrying heavy burdens?
- Praying or reading your Bible are ways to "come to Jesus." What are other ways you can do this?
- Do you ever find that "coming to Jesus" is hard to do? Why or why not?
- What does Jesus promise to do for you if you come to him?
- After reading this passage, what is one new word that you would use to describe Jesus?

Hanging out with God
- Did you know that you can rest with God? Resting is even something that God did. Do you remember what God did on the seventh day of creation? He rested! (Check out Genesis 2:2.)
- Take the next couple of moments to tell God anything that might be causing you stress. Then rest with God: Lie on the couch, turn on a worship song, take a nap in your bed, or—if it's warm out—grab a blanket and lay out in the sunshine. God WANTS to give you rest! How cool is that?!

This space is here for you to jot down some thoughts, write out a prayer, draw a picture, or do whatever you want to help you remember your 10-minute moment.

Day 9

AFRAID IN A STORM

Think of the scariest thing you've ever seen. If it was scary enough that you thought you might die, you'll know how Jesus' disciples felt in this Red Stuff. They were seriously afraid that they were going to drown. As they traveled with Jesus across a big lake, a storm came up with high waves that freaked them out. The crazy part is that when they looked at Jesus, he was asleep! Sometimes the challenges in our life can be as scary as a raging thunderstorm on a lake in a boat, and we wonder if we're going to make it. But read what happens when the disciples realized that it makes a difference when you know that Jesus is WITH you!

2 MINUTES

Read the passage below. Circle or underline any words/phrases/ verses that you feel are important to remember.

Mark 4:35-41 (NLT) (You can also read Matthew's account in Matthew 8:23-27 and Luke's account in Luke 8:22-25.)

35 As evening came, Jesus said to his disciples, "Let's cross to the other side of the lake." 36 So they took Jesus in the boat and started out, leaving the crowds behind (although other boats followed). 37 But soon a fierce storm came up. High waves were breaking into the boat, and it began to fill with water.

38 Jesus was sleeping at the back of the boat with his head on a cushion. The disciples woke him up, shouting, "Teacher, don't you care that we're going to drown?"

³⁹ When Jesus woke up, he rebuked the wind and said to the waves, "Silence! Be still!" Suddenly the wind stopped, and there was a great calm. ⁴⁰ Then he asked them, "Why are you afraid? Do you still have no faith?"

⁴¹ The disciples were absolutely terrified. "Who is this man?" they asked each other. "Even the wind and waves obey him!"

Think about the following questions and how they might apply to your life.
- What's the first thought that comes to your mind after reading this passage?
- If you were one of the disciples on the boat, how do you think you would have responded?
- Have you ever been in a situation where you felt overwhelmed, scared, or alone? Where were you, and what happened?
- Do you think the disciples learned anything from this experience? If so, what do you think they learned?
- You might not be caught on a boat in a storm anytime soon, but sometimes the most unexpected things can show up in life. When they do, what can you remember from this passage?

Hanging out with God
- God is always with us, even when it feels like he's not. Think of two or three incidents from your life when you felt scared. If you could go back in time and be 100% certain God was with you, would that have changed the way you felt or acted? Explain.
- Take a minute to thank God for his presence in your life.

THOUGHTS

This space is here for you to jot down some thoughts, write out a prayer, draw a picture, or do whatever you want to help you remember your 10-minute moment.

AFRAID IN A STORM... AGAIN

Day 10

Like yesterday's passage from the Bible, the disciples are in a boat crossing a lake. But this time, Jesus sent them ahead without him, telling them he'd meet them on the other side. It was night, and the lake again got stormy. (Rough weather on this lake!) In the middle of the storm, the disciples can't believe their eyes. They see a person walking across the lake, on top of the water! (Sounds like an episode of "Scooby Doo" or something.) After Peter realizes that it's actually Jesus coming toward them, Jesus asks him to do the craziest thing: Step out of the boat and walk on the water with him! Jesus knows it's going to take courage to do so. Is there anything courageous Jesus has asked you to do lately? Keep that in mind as you read this section of The Red Stuff!

2 MINUTES

Read the passage below. Circle or underline any words/phrases/ verses that you feel are important to remember.

Matthew 14:22-33 (NLT) (You can also read Mark's account in Mark 6:45-56 and John's account in John 6:16-21.)

22 Immediately after this, Jesus insisted that his disciples get back into the boat and cross to the other side of the lake, while he sent the people home. 23 After sending them home, he went up into the hills by himself to pray. Night fell while he was there alone.

24 Meanwhile, the disciples were in trouble far away from land, for a strong wind had risen, and they were fighting heavy waves.

25 About three o'clock in the morning Jesus came toward them, walking on the water. 26 When the disciples saw him walking on the water, they were terrified. In their fear, they cried out, "It's a ghost!"

27 But Jesus spoke to them at once. "Don't be afraid," he said. "Take courage. I am here!"

28 Then Peter called to him, "Lord, if it's really you, tell me to come to you, walking on the water."

29 "Yes, come," Jesus said.

So Peter went over the side of the boat and walked on the water toward Jesus. 30 But when he saw the strong wind and the waves, he was terrified and began to sink. "Save me, Lord!" he shouted.

31 Jesus immediately reached out and grabbed him. "You have so little faith," Jesus said. "Why did you doubt me?"

32 When they climbed back into the boat, the wind stopped. 33 Then the disciples worshiped him. "You really are the Son of God!" they exclaimed.

Think about the following questions and how they might apply to your life.

- What has Jesus asked you to do lately that required courage? There's probably something!
- Just like the disciples in verses 26-27, if someone needs courage, it means that person is afraid of something. Is there something that you are facing in your life that you are afraid of? If so, what is it?
- Peter's response in verse 28 is interesting. Why do you think he said that?
- This passage tells us that the disciples were afraid. What does it tell us about how Jesus might have felt? Why do you think he might have felt that way?

- Sometimes when we face big situations that might scare us, it's easier to focus on the situation than on Jesus and who he is. What can you learn from Jesus' responses in verse 27 and verse 31?

Hanging out with God
- Pray and ask God if there is something he wants you to do that would take courage. Sit in silence for a minute, and see if he brings anything to mind. If so, ask God to remind you of this passage if you feel afraid.
- Then take that step of courage—and do it!

This space is here for you to jot down some thoughts, write out a prayer, draw a picture, or do whatever you want to help you remember your 10-minute moment.

Day 11 — WHEN YOU'RE SO MAD AT SOMEBODY

Everybody gets mad sometimes! Even the kind of anger that makes you grit your teeth, or maybe growl, or even want to kick the dog. (But don't kick the dog—it won't help.) Some people think it's a sin to get angry, but it's not! Even Jesus got angry. But there are two things to remember when you're angry. First, Ephesians 4:26 says, "In your anger, do not sin." God knows we're going to get angry; he just doesn't want us to sin in the process. And second, this section of The Red Stuff tells what to do when we're mad at somebody. Sometimes we get so mad with someone that we just stop talking to this person, or we decide to bury the friendship. Jesus says there's a better way to deal with anger. Read on!

Read the passage below. Circle or underline any words/phrases/verses that you feel are important to remember.

Matthew 5:21-26 (NLT)
21 "You have heard that our ancestors were told, 'You must not murder. If you commit murder, you are subject to judgment.'
22 But I say, if you are even angry with someone, you are subject to judgment! If you call someone an idiot, you are in danger of being brought before the court. And if you curse someone, you are in danger of the fires of hell.

23 "So if you are presenting a sacrifice at the altar in the Temple and you suddenly remember that someone has something against you,
24 leave your sacrifice there at the altar. Go and be reconciled to that person. Then come and offer your sacrifice to God.

25 *"When you are on the way to court with your adversary, settle your differences quickly. Otherwise, your accuser may hand you over to the judge, who will hand you over to an officer, and you will be thrown into prison. 26 And if that happens, you surely won't be free again until you have paid the last penny."*

Think about the following questions and how they might apply to your life.

- Who was the last person that made you so angry you wanted to growl? What happened? How did you respond? Do you still talk to that person? Why or why not?
- In verses 21-22, Jesus talks about the dangers of our anger, name-calling, and cursing. What are some of the risks? What do you think about that?
- What are two ways you can honor God when you get angry with other people?
- In verses 23-24, Jesus tells us that if you are going to church to worship him and realize someone has something against you, it's important to go deal with the issue. Why do you think it's important to leave first and then come back to worship (instead of just "doing it later")?
- It's always good to check our hearts with God and make sure there's nothing we are trying to hide from him. God wants us to come before him with a pure heart. Is there anyone in your life that you might have something against—or someone who might have something against you?

Hanging out with God
- Is there someone that comes to mind who might have something against you, or be really ticked at you for something you did? Is there something that you need to do to make it right?
- Spend the next 3 minutes with God and share the situation with him. Confess any sins you might have committed in the situation and ask God to forgive you. See if there's anything he wants you to do.

THOUGHTS

This space is here for you to jot down some thoughts, write out a prayer, draw a picture, or do whatever you want to help you remember your 10-minute moment.

Day 12
DON'T WORRY

Jesus' words are so cool, especially when you're worrying about something. In this Red Stuff, Jesus wants you to grasp how huge and deep his love and care are for you. He pays attention to every detail of your life and wants you to trust him with every little part, from your food and clothes, to your friendships and challenges, all the way to your eternity. When someone says "don't worry," it's easy to think "you have no idea what I'm going through—or else you'd know why I'm so worried." But Jesus does know, and he promises that he'll get you through it!

Read the passage below. Circle or underline any words/phrases/verses that you feel are important to remember.

Matthew 6:25-34 (NLT)

25 "That is why I tell you not to worry about everyday life—whether you have enough food and drink, or enough clothes to wear. Isn't life more than food, and your body more than clothing? 26 Look at the birds. They don't plant or harvest or store food in barns, for your heavenly Father feeds them. And aren't you far more valuable to him than they are? 27 Can all your worries add a single moment to your life?

28 "And why worry about your clothing? Look at the lilies of the field and how they grow. They don't work or make their clothing, 29 yet Solomon in all his glory was not dressed as beautifully as they are.

³⁰ *And if God cares so wonderfully for wildflowers that are here today and thrown into the fire tomorrow, he will certainly care for you. Why do you have so little faith?*

³¹ *"So don't worry about these things, saying, 'What will we eat? What will we drink? What will we wear?'* ³² *These things dominate the thoughts of unbelievers, but your heavenly Father already knows all your needs.* ³³ *Seek the Kingdom of God above all else, and live righteously, and he will give you everything you need.*

³⁴ *"So don't worry about tomorrow, for tomorrow will bring its own worries. Today's trouble is enough for today."*

Think about the following questions and how they might apply to your life.
- What is one new thing you learned from this passage? It could be about your relationship with God, something about Jesus, a situation you are dealing with, or something else.
- Jesus encourages us not to worry about everyday life, but rather trust in God and he will take care of you. What are the two examples Jesus uses to make this point in verses 26-30?
- At one time or another, we all catch ourselves worrying about something in our lives. What is something that you worry about?
- In verse 33, what two steps does Jesus tell us to take when we worry? How might this look in your life?
- In the same verse, did you notice that God promises to "give you everything you need"? Jesus didn't say that God would give us everything we want but everything we need. What are examples in your life of something you want and something you need?

Hanging out with God
- Spend the next couple of minutes sharing some of your worries with God. What are you worried or anxious about? Why do you think you are worried or anxious about it?

- Share your worries with God. God has endless wisdom and wants to give us peace during stressful times. Ask God to give you wisdom and peace when you start to worry.

This space is here for you to jot down some thoughts, write out a prayer, draw a picture, or do whatever you want to help you remember your 10-minute moment.

Day 13

FIRST DISCIPLES

Have you ever been "chosen" for something? Maybe for a sports team, or for the cast of a play, or something else? It's a pretty good feeling. Today we're talking about the power of Jesus' words to call people to follow him—to become his disciples. These guys were chosen by Jesus to help him begin a world-changing ministry that's still rocking things 2,000 years later. But the Bible tells us that these were ordinary guys, not so different from you. Spend today thinking about the disciples' commitment to follow Jesus, as well as what it means for you to follow him, too.

Read the passage below. Circle or underline any words/phrases/ verses that you feel are important to remember.

Mark 1:16-20 (NLT) (You can also read Matthew's version in Matthew 4:18-22.)

¹⁶ One day as Jesus was walking along the shore of the Sea of Galilee, he saw Simon (also called Peter) and his brother Andrew throwing a net into the water, for they fished for a living. ¹⁷ Jesus called out to them, "Come, follow me, and I will show you how to fish for people!" ¹⁸ And they left their nets at once and followed him.

¹⁹ A little farther up the shore Jesus saw Zebedee's sons, James and John, in a boat repairing their nets. ²⁰ He called them at once, and they also followed him, leaving their father, Zebedee, in the boat with the hired men."

Think about the following questions and how they might apply to your life.

- Can you imagine being in Simon and Andrew's shoes? How crazy would it be if Jesus walked up to you and simply asked you to follow him? What would you have done?
- From these verses, do you think any of the four guys who followed Jesus that day really knew what they were getting into? Imagine how compelling Jesus' invitation was!
- How do you think James and John's father, Zebedee, reacted to this news?
- Imagine this: Simon, Andrew, James and John were the very first followers of Jesus! If you have chosen to follow Jesus, what made you decide that you wanted to become his follower?
- How has being a follower of Jesus affected your life?

Hanging out with God

- God deeply cares about and desires to have a relationship with every single person! If you have already decided to follow Jesus, use this time to thank him for his invitation. Let God know why this relationship is important to you!
- If you haven't invited Jesus into your life, it's important to know that his offer always stands. Find a trusted friend or adult who knows Jesus and talk to this person about your desire. Or on your own, you can simply tell God that you want to have a relationship with him. Let God know that you believe Jesus died for your sins and you want him to lead your life. It's that simple…and it's life-changing! Be sure to share this great news with someone!

THOUGHTS

This space is here for you to jot down some thoughts, write out a prayer, draw a picture, or do whatever you want to help you remember your 10-minute moment.

Day 14

PURE ON THE INSIDE

In Jesus' day, the Pharisees were religious leaders who appeared to be holy and interested in spiritual things. We say that they "appeared" that way because they were primarily concerned with how things looked and whether or not the rules were followed. But Jesus was more interested in what was going on INSIDE a person. When Jesus speaks The Red Stuff in this chapter, he quotes an important section of the Old Testament: "These people honor me with their lips, but their hearts are far from me." As you read, think about what Jesus was trying to get the Pharisees to understand.

Read the passage below. Circle or underline any words/phrases/ verses that you feel are important to remember.

Mark 7:1-15 (NLT) (You can also read Matthew's version of this in Matthew 15:1-20.)

¹ One day some Pharisees and teachers of religious law arrived from Jerusalem to see Jesus. ² They noticed that some of his disciples failed to follow the Jewish ritual of hand washing before eating. ³ (The Jews, especially the Pharisees, do not eat until they have poured water over their cupped hands, as required by their ancient traditions. ⁴ Similarly, they don't eat anything from the market until they immerse their hands in water. This is but one of many traditions they have clung to—such as their ceremonial washing of cups, pitchers, and kettles.)

5 So the Pharisees and teachers of religious law asked him, "Why don't your disciples follow our age-old tradition? They eat without first performing the hand-washing ceremony."

6 Jesus replied, "You hypocrites! Isaiah was right when he prophesied about you, for he wrote,
  'These people honor me with their lips,
  but their hearts are far from me.
  7 Their worship is a farce,
  for they teach man-made ideas as commands from God.'

8 For you ignore God's law and substitute your own tradition."

9 Then he said, "You skillfully sidestep God's law in order to hold on to your own tradition. *10* For instance, Moses gave you this law from God: 'Honor your father and mother,' and 'Anyone who speaks disrespectfully of father or mother must be put to death.' *11* But you say it is all right for people to say to their parents, 'Sorry, I can't help you. For I have vowed to give to God what I would have given to you.' *12* In this way, you let them disregard their needy parents. *13* And so you cancel the word of God in order to hand down your own tradition. And this is only one example among many others."

14 Then Jesus called to the crowd to come and hear. "All of you listen," he said, "and try to understand. *15* It's not what goes into your body that defiles you; you are defiled by what comes from your heart."

Think about the following questions and how they might apply to your life.
- Wow—this is a side of Jesus we haven't seen before! What are three words you would use to describe Jesus, after reading this passage?
- Did you see the verses where Jesus quotes the Old Testament? What did they say? The book of Isaiah was written hundreds of years earlier, and Jesus said that it was applicable to these Pharisees. Check it out yourself in Isaiah 29:13.
- Describe in your own words what a "hypocrite" is. Have you ever been hypocritical? If so, how?

- Jesus cares more about what was going on inside a person (their heart) than whether or not they were rule followers. Why do you think this is important?

Hanging out with God
- Spend the next 3 minutes talking with God. Share with him anything that may be on your heart. Confess any stuff you've done wrong—or maybe times you have been hypocritical—and ask for forgiveness. He'll forgive you!

This space is here for you to jot down some thoughts, write out a prayer, draw a picture, or do whatever you want to help you remember your 10-minute moment.

Day 15 — PETER GETS A NEW NAME

Do you know anyone with a nickname? Not just a shortened version of a real name, but a nickname that someone has given this person because of a quality or trait. Like "Shooter" for someone who's good at basketball, or "Lightning" for someone who's fast. Or you've probably heard people call someone by a nickname that just sounds plain mean. In this section of The Red Stuff, Jesus gives Peter a new name. Names had an extra measure of importance during Jesus' days on earth, because they represented something significant about the person. So when Jesus told Peter he was giving him a new name—it was a big deal. Jesus wanted Peter to see himself not only for who he was, but for who he could be. As you read this, imagine what Peter was thinking when Jesus gave him this new name.

Read the passage below. Circle or underline any words/phrases/verses that you feel are important to remember.

Matthew 16:13-19 (NLT)

13 When Jesus came to the region of Caesarea Philippi, he asked his disciples, "Who do people say that the Son of Man is?"

14 "Well," they replied, "some say John the Baptist, some say Elijah, and others say Jeremiah or one of the other prophets."

15 Then he asked them, "But who do you say I am?"

16 Simon Peter answered, "You are the Messiah, the Son of the living God."

17 Jesus replied, "You are blessed, Simon son of John, because my Father in heaven has revealed this to you. You did not learn this from any human being. 18 Now I say to you that you are Peter (which means 'rock'), and upon this rock I will build my church, and all the powers of hell will not conquer it. 19 And I will give you the keys of the Kingdom of Heaven. Whatever you forbid on earth will be forbidden in heaven, and whatever you permit on earth will be permitted in heaven."

Think about the following questions and how they might apply to your life.
- If you were to ask your friends who Jesus is, what do you think they would say?
- If someone asked you who Jesus is, what would you say? How would you describe Jesus to others?
- How do you think Peter felt when Jesus gave him a new name?
- What does the name "Peter" mean? What did Jesus say that Peter would do in the future?
- If Jesus were to give you a new name, what name might he choose?

Hanging out with God
- There's something powerful in a nickname! Spend the next three minutes and make a list of all of the nicknames Jesus was given in the Bible. For example: Son of God, Bread of Life, Prince of Peace, The Way, The Truth, The Life. What can you add?
- What nickname would you give Jesus that reflects his activity in your life? Explain the name.

THOUGHTS

This space is here for you to jot down some thoughts, write out a prayer, draw a picture, or do whatever you want to help you remember your 10-minute moment.

WHEN SOMEONE HURTS YOU

Day 16

If you're going to be in relationship with people, sooner or later you're going to get hurt. That's not big news, but what is big news is how Jesus says we can deal with pain in friendships. This section of The Red Stuff basically lays out a "three-step plan" for responding when somebody does you wrong. It's not like a math formula, but these steps work! Interestingly, the first step is probably the one most of us skip. If more people did Matthew 18:15 the way that it's written, there'd be a lot less pain.

Read the passage below. Circle or underline any words/phrases/ verses that you feel are important to remember.

Matthew 18:15-20 (NLT)
¹⁵ *"If another believer sins against you, go privately and point out the offense. If the other person listens and confesses it, you have won that person back. ¹⁶ But if you are unsuccessful, take one or two others with you and go back again, so that everything you say may be confirmed by two or three witnesses. ¹⁷ If the person still refuses to listen, take your case to the church. Then if he or she won't accept the church's decision, treat that person as a pagan or a corrupt tax collector.*

¹⁸ *"I tell you the truth, whatever you forbid on earth will be forbidden in heaven, and whatever you permit on earth will be permitted in heaven.*

19 "I also tell you this: If two of you agree here on earth concerning anything you ask, my Father in heaven will do it for you. 20 For where two or three gather together as my followers, I am there among them."

Think about the following questions and how they might apply to your life.

- Describe a time when someone hurt you. How did you feel? What did you do?
- What does Jesus say you should do if someone sins against you or hurts you?
- In verse 15, Jesus tells us that it's important for us to go to the person privately when we've been hurt. Have you ever skipped this step and told others first? In what ways can that be harmful?
- Why do you think Jesus tells us we should first go to the person who wronged us? Why do you think he tells us to go privately? Is this hard for you to do? Why?
- Think about a time you were wronged. If you follow Jesus' instructions the next time someone hurts you, how do you think these steps would work?

Hanging out with God

- As you spend the next couple of minutes with God, can you think of a situation when you've been hurt and still struggle with it?
- Pray and share with God what happened and how you feel. Ask God what your next steps might be and if you need to talk with this person. It might be tough to have a conversation, but Jesus knew what he was talking about when he shared these verses with us. If you are scared, ask God to give you wisdom with the words that you are going to say and strength to do what is right.

THOUGHTS

This space is here for you to jot down some thoughts, write out a prayer, draw a picture, or do whatever you want to help you remember your 10-minute moment.

Day 17   TOO BUSY?

This is a fascinating bit of Red Stuff, about two sisters: One running around like crazy, helping get stuff done, and the other sister "just sitting there" but listening to Jesus talk. Martha, the first sister, believes she's doing the right thing; you get the sense that she's hustling to get everything prepared, while Mary, the other sister, looks a little lazy. So Martha "tells on" Mary. I imagine her saying in a whiny voice, "Jesus! Tell Mary to stop being lazy, and to help me." But Jesus' response might surprise you. His words show that there's one "most important" thing, and sometimes we can be so busy that we miss it.

Read the passage below. Circle or underline any words/phrases/ verses that you feel are important to remember.

Luke 10:38-42 (NLT)
38 As Jesus and the disciples continued on their way to Jerusalem, they came to a certain village where a woman named Martha welcomed him into her home. 39 Her sister, Mary, sat at the Lord's feet, listening to what he taught. 40 But Martha was distracted by the big dinner she was preparing. She came to Jesus and said, "Lord, doesn't it seem unfair to you that my sister just sits here while I do all the work? Tell her to come and help me."

41 But the Lord said to her, "My dear Martha, you are worried and upset over all these details! 42 There is only one thing worth being concerned about. Mary has discovered it, and it will not be taken away from her."

Think about the following questions and how they might apply to your life.

- This is a classic example of a relationship between two siblings. Even if you don't have a brother or sister, can you relate to this experience?
- What was Martha doing in this passage? What was Mary doing in this passage? If you had to choose, do you think you are more like Martha or Mary? Why?
- In verse 41, what was Jesus' response to Martha's statement? What did Jesus say about Mary's actions (in verse 42)?
- There are lots of things we can do during the day. Make a list of all the things that you do in a typical day (for example, get up, eat breakfast, brush your teeth, feed the dog, get dressed, make your bed). Where does God fit into your day? How might you build your day around God?
- Jesus says in verse 42 that Mary is doing the best thing; what is she doing? How often do you sit and just listen to God or read what he has to say in the Bible? Why do you think it might be important to be like Mary?

Hanging out with God
- If the weather is nice outside, spend the next 3 minutes outdoors with God, maybe lying in the grass or walking around or swinging on a swing—anything!
- Jesus said the best thing we can do is to sit and listen to him. Close your eyes; what do you hear? Open your eyes; what do you see? God is the maker of all creation! As you listen and look around, invite God to show you his creation—and to help you not let "things" get in the way of hearing him today.

THOUGHTS

This space is here for you to jot down some thoughts, write out a prayer, draw a picture, or do whatever you want to help you remember your 10-minute moment.

Day 18
HEARING JESUS' VOICE

Think about all the voices you hear in a single day—probably lots and lots of them—some you know and many you don't. Yet sometimes when you answer the phone, there are people who only have to say, "It's me!" and you know exactly who "me" is. Why? Because you're familiar with the voice. You've spent so much time listening to it that you instantly recognize it. In this section of The Red Stuff, Jesus compares us to sheep and himself to a shepherd. If you're really a "follower" of Jesus, it means that you start to get good at "recognizing his voice" and following where that voice leads you.

2 MINUTES

Read the passage below. Circle or underline any words/phrases/verses that you feel are important to remember.

John 10:1-16 (NLT)
¹ "I tell you the truth, anyone who sneaks over the wall of a sheepfold, rather than going through the gate, must surely be a thief and a robber! ² But the one who enters through the gate is the shepherd of the sheep. ³ The gatekeeper opens the gate for him, and the sheep recognize his voice and come to him. He calls his own sheep by name and leads them out. ⁴ After he has gathered his own flock, he walks ahead of them, and they follow him because they know his voice. ⁵ They won't follow a stranger; they will run from him because they don't know his voice."

⁶ Those who heard Jesus use this illustration didn't understand what he meant, ⁷ so he explained it to them: "I tell you the truth, I am the gate for the sheep. ⁸ All who came before me were thieves and robbers. But the true sheep did not listen to them.

⁹ Yes, I am the gate. Those who come in through me will be saved. They will come and go freely and will find good pastures. ¹⁰ The thief's purpose is to steal and kill and destroy. My purpose is to give them a rich and satisfying life.

¹¹ "I am the good shepherd. The good shepherd sacrifices his life for the sheep. ¹² A hired hand will run when he sees a wolf coming. He will abandon the sheep because they don't belong to him and he isn't their shepherd. And so the wolf attacks them and scatters the flock. ¹³ The hired hand runs away because he's working only for the money and doesn't really care about the sheep.

¹⁴ "I am the good shepherd; I know my own sheep, and they know me, ¹⁵ just as my Father knows me and I know the Father. So I sacrifice my life for the sheep. ¹⁶ I have other sheep, too, that are not in this sheepfold. I must bring them also. They will listen to my voice, and there will be one flock with one shepherd."

5 MINUTES

Think about the following questions and how they might apply to your life.

- In this illustration, Jesus talks first about a thief and robber—the enemy of the sheep and shepherd. Then he reveals that he is the Good Shepherd. Who do you think the thief and robber represent?
- Compared to sheep listening to their shepherd, do you think it's important for us to be able to recognize the voice of Jesus, our Good Shepherd? Why or why not?
- Describe a time that you have struggled with hearing or listening to the "voice" of Jesus. Why do you think it was hard? Describe a time that you did listen to the voice of Jesus. What happened?
- If you don't hear Jesus' audible voice speaking, how else might he be speaking into your life? What are other ways you might hear his voice?
- In your own life, how do you determine if you're hearing Jesus' voice or the voice of a thief or robber?

- Recognizing the voice of Jesus can be really tough sometimes. But just like a good friend, the more you get to know someone, the more you recognize that person's voice. What are one or two different ways you could try to better recognize Jesus' voice?

Hanging out with God
- Is there a situation in your life right now where you could really use Jesus' help? Share the situation with him and see if there's anything he wants to say to you. Then spend a couple minutes listening for his voice. Maybe he wants to say something to you right now!

This space is here for you to jot down some thoughts, write out a prayer, draw a picture, or do whatever you want to help you remember your 10-minute moment.

THE LOST SHEEP & THE LOST COIN

Day 19

Did you ever lose something that you really valued? Losing stuff is a drag! In these two stories, Jesus describes something of great value that is missing. In the first story a shepherd loses a sheep; in the second story a woman loses a coin. The interesting thing is that the shepherd has 99 other sheep, and the lady has nine other coins. But for some reason, the one that's missing causes both of them to stop everything and call out a search party. Maybe you've heard people who don't follow Jesus referred to as "lost." Notice what happens when the coin and the sheep get "found!"

Read the passage below. Circle or underline any words/phrases/ verses that you feel are important to remember.

Luke 15:1-10 (NLT) (You can also read Matthew's account in Matthew 18:12-14.)

¹ Tax collectors and other notorious sinners often came to listen to Jesus teach. ² This made the Pharisees and teachers of religious law complain that he was associating with such sinful people—even eating with them!

³ So Jesus told them this story: ⁴ "If a man has a hundred sheep and one of them gets lost, what will he do? Won't he leave the ninety-nine others in the wilderness and go to search for the one that is lost until he finds it? ⁵ And when he has found it, he will joyfully carry it home on his shoulders. ⁶ When he arrives, he will call together his friends and neighbors, saying, 'Rejoice with me because I have found my lost sheep.' [7] *In the same way, there is more joy in heaven over one lost sinner who repents and returns to God than over ninety-nine others who are righteous and haven't strayed away!*

[8] *"Or suppose a woman has ten silver coins and loses one. Won't she light a lamp and sweep the entire house and search carefully until she finds it?* [9] *And when she finds it, she will call in her friends and neighbors and say, 'Rejoice with me because I have found my lost coin.'* [10] *In the same way, there is joy in the presence of God's angels when even one sinner repents."*

Think about the following questions and how they might apply to your life.

- Jesus is trying to make a point with both of these stories. What similarities do you see between the story of the lost sheep and the story of the lost coin?
- What did the man who lost his sheep and the woman who lost her coin do when they realized they were missing their belongings?
- Why do you think it was so important that they find the lost sheep and the lost coin?
- Did you notice how they responded when they found what was lost? What did they do? What do you think that means about the value of what was lost?
- From what you've seen in this passage, how do you think God feels about people who are "lost" (those who don't know him)?
- How do you think God feels when people come to know him and begin a relationship with him?

Hanging out with God

Let's do a heart check to see if our heart matches with God's heart.

- Invite God into this time and share your thoughts with him about this passage. Maybe celebrate that God never gives up searching for his lost children. Thank God for being one who parties when someone begins a relationship with him.
- Think about people in your life who don't know God. Does the way you feel about these people reflect the way God feels about these people? If not, ask God to give you his heart for them!

This space is here for you to jot down some thoughts, write out a prayer, draw a picture, or do whatever you want to help you remember your 10-minute moment.

Day 20

THE LOST SON

So losing some money or an animal would be a bummer, right? But this story takes it to another level; it's about losing a person. In this Red Stuff, Jesus tells about a son who decides that he's had enough of living under dad's rules, and he moves out. But he's such a wild spender that he ends up with nothing left. Like yesterday's passage, pay close attention to what happens when the person who lost something reacts. (This time it's the father, who "lost" his son.) The father in this story represents God and how he feels about YOU!

Read the passage below. Circle or underline any words/phrases/ verses that you feel are important to remember.

Luke 15:11-24 (NLT)
11 To illustrate the point further, Jesus told them this story: "A man had two sons. 12 The younger son told his father, 'I want my share of your estate now before you die.' So his father agreed to divide his wealth between his sons.

13 "A few days later this younger son packed all his belongings and moved to a distant land, and there he wasted all his money in wild living. 14 About the time his money ran out, a great famine swept over the land, and he began to starve. 15 He persuaded a local farmer to hire him, and the man sent him into his fields to feed the pigs. 16 The young man became so hungry that even the pods he was feeding the pigs looked good to him. But no one gave him anything.

17 *"When he finally came to his senses, he said to himself, 'At home even the hired servants have food enough to spare, and here I am dying of hunger! 18 I will go home to my father and say, "Father, I have sinned against both heaven and you, 19 and I am no longer worthy of being called your son. Please take me on as a hired servant."'*

20 *"So he returned home to his father. And while he was still a long way off, his father saw him coming. Filled with love and compassion, he ran to his son, embraced him, and kissed him. 21 His son said to him, 'Father, I have sinned against both heaven and you, and I am no longer worthy of being called your son.'*

22 *"But his father said to the servants, 'Quick! Bring the finest robe in the house and put it on him. Get a ring for his finger and sandals for his feet. 23 And kill the calf we have been fattening. We must celebrate with a feast, 24 for this son of mine was dead and has now returned to life. He was lost, but now he is found.' So the party began.*

5 MINUTES

Think about the following questions and how they might apply to your life.

- Jesus tells yet another story about someone losing something. Seems like Jesus is really trying to make a point! Look back at the stories of the lost sheep and the lost coin and see if you can find similarities and differences between those two passages and this one. Why do you think Jesus added a third "lost and found" story? Why do you think this one was important to share?
- Have you ever disagreed with or disobeyed your parents? If so, what was it about?
- When the younger son realized he was wrong, what did he do in verses 17-19? Describe a time when you were wrong and needed to apologize to your parents. How did they respond to your apology?
- What was the father's reaction in verses 20-24? Does this surprise you? If you were the father, how do you think you might have reacted?

- In these verses, the father represents God and the younger son represents each one of us. When you make that connection, what thoughts do you have about your relationship with God?

Hanging out with God
- It's pretty cool to see how God thinks of us and how he responds to us, even during our "not so good" moments. Spend this time thanking God for who he is and what he has done for you.

This space is here for you to jot down some thoughts, write out a prayer, draw a picture, or do whatever you want to help you remember your 10-minute moment.

Day 21

JESUS TALKS ABOUT DIVORCE

This is a painful topic. Despite the zillions of Hollywood movies celebrating love, romance, and marriage, sometimes marriages don't last. Divorce may have happened in your own family, or in a friend's family. But what does God say about divorce? In the Old Testament book of Malachi 2:6, God says "I hate divorce." Wow—strong statement. You may have heard adults say "it's complicated" when it comes to divorce, and it is. But God is pretty clear about how long he intended a marriage to last: a lifetime. Imagine sticking two pieces of different colored, already-chewed bubble gum together in a wad, and then trying to pull the two pieces apart. Almost impossible to do—and if gum could feel pain, it would probably hurt! As you read today's Red Stuff, pray for those you know who are dealing with the pain of divorce. God cares!

2 MINUTES

Read the passage below. Circle or underline any words/phrases/ verses that you feel are important to remember.

Matthew 19:1-8 (NLT) (You can also read Mark's account in Mark 10:1-9.)

1 When Jesus had finished saying these things, he left Galilee and went down to the region of Judea east of the Jordan River. 2 Large crowds followed him there, and he healed their sick.

3 Some Pharisees came and tried to trap him with this question: "Should a man be allowed to divorce his wife for just any reason?"

4 "Haven't you read the Scriptures?" Jesus replied. "They record that from the beginning 'God made them male and female.' *5* And he said, 'This explains why a man leaves his father and mother and is joined to his wife, and the two are united into one.' *6* Since they are no longer two but one, let no one split apart what God has joined together."

7 "Then why did Moses say in the law that a man could give his wife a written notice of divorce and send her away?" they asked.

8 Jesus replied, "Moses permitted divorce only as a concession to your hard hearts, but it was not what God had originally intended."

Think about the following questions and how they might apply to your life.
- In your own words, explain what Jesus says about divorce.
- In verses 4-6, what does it say is God's role in marriage?
- Have you ever experienced divorce in your family, or do you have friends who have gone through it? What was your experience? How did it make you feel?
- Have you ever shared with God your feelings and experience with divorce? Why or why not? Do you think he cares? If so, how do you know?

Hanging out with God
- God never turns his back on you and never grows tired of hearing your voice. Never! Spend the next 3 minutes sharing with God whatever you're feeling right now. He wants you to know that he is close to you.

TH●UGHTS

This space is here for you to jot down some thoughts, write out a prayer, draw a picture, or do whatever you want to help you remember your 10-minute moment.

Day 22

LEADING BY... SERVING?

Did you ever know people who thought they could be important by being close to someone who was important? That's one of the reasons why there's such a fascination with celebrities. People figure if they can get next to someone famous, then maybe others will admire them, too. But once again, Jesus turns things upside down in The Red Stuff. James and John (who are brothers) come right out and ask Jesus if they can hang out right next to him and share the spotlight with him. (They didn't realize the spotlight would get messy when Jesus was crucified!) But Jesus tells them that being great required a completely different way of thinking.

2 MINUTES

Read the passage below. Circle or underline any words/phrases/ verses that you feel are important to remember.

Mark 10:35-45 (NLT) (You can also read Matthew's version in Matthew 20:20-28.)

35 Then James and John, the sons of Zebedee, came over and spoke to him. "Teacher," they said, "we want you to do us a favor."

36 "What is your request?" he asked.

37 They replied, "When you sit on your glorious throne, we want to sit in places of honor next to you, one on your right and the other on your left."

³⁸ But Jesus said to them, "You don't know what you are asking! Are you able to drink from the bitter cup of suffering I am about to drink? Are you able to be baptized with the baptism of suffering I must be baptized with?"

³⁹ "Oh yes," they replied, "we are able!"

Then Jesus told them, "You will indeed drink from my bitter cup and be baptized with my baptism of suffering. ⁴⁰ But I have no right to say who will sit on my right or my left. God has prepared those places for the ones he has chosen."

⁴¹ When the ten other disciples heard what James and John had asked, they were indignant. ⁴² So Jesus called them together and said, "You know that the rulers in this world lord it over their people, and officials flaunt their authority over those under them. ⁴³ But among you it will be different. Whoever wants to be a leader among you must be your servant, ⁴⁴ and whoever wants to be first among you must be the slave of everyone else. ⁴⁵ For even the Son of Man came not to be served but to serve others and to give his life as a ransom for many."

5 MINUTES

Think about the following questions and how they might apply to your life.

- Read Matthew 20:20-28 for his account of this story, and identify similarities and differences in the two passages.
- James and John had a major request for Jesus in Mark 10:37. What was your reaction when you read it?
- What do you think Jesus was talking about in verse 38? Do you think James and John fully understood that Jesus was talking about his upcoming crucifixion? Why or why not?
- Jesus turns things upside down in verses 43-45. In your own words, explain what you think Jesus means by this.
- What do you think it would look like to live out verses 43-45 in your own life right now? Is there anything that would stop you from doing that right away? If so, what?

Hanging out with God

- In verses 43-44, Jesus makes it clear that he wants us to lead by serving others. Spend 3 minutes talking to God about what you could do to grow as a servant and leader at school, at church, or at home.

This space is here for you to jot down some thoughts, write out a prayer, draw a picture, or do whatever you want to help you remember your 10-minute moment.

WHAT TO DO WITH THE TALENTS GOD GIVES YOU

Jesus loves to tell stories in The Red Stuff, and here's another one. But as usual, Jesus wants to make a point that's bigger than just an interesting story. There are a couple of things to think about as you read this story. The person in these verses called "Master" or "King" represents God. The "servants" who get the silver represent you and me. Just keep in mind that the "silver" that gets handed out isn't actually silver, but it represents the talents and abilities that God has given to each of us.

2 MINUTES

Read the passage below. Circle or underline any words/phrases/ verses that you feel are important to remember.

Luke 19:11-27 (NLT)

¹¹ The crowd was listening to everything Jesus said. And because he was nearing Jerusalem, he told them a story to correct the impression that the Kingdom of God would begin right away. ¹² He said, "A nobleman was called away to a distant empire to be crowned king and then return. ¹³ Before he left, he called together ten of his servants and divided among them ten pounds of silver, saying, 'Invest this for me while I am gone.' ¹⁴ But his people hated him and sent a delegation after him to say, 'We do not want him to be our king.'

¹⁵ "After he was crowned king, he returned and called in the servants to whom he had given the money. He wanted to find out what their profits were. ¹⁶ The first servant reported, 'Master, I invested your money and made ten times the original amount!'

¹⁷ "'Well done!' the king exclaimed. 'You are a good servant. You have been faithful with the little I entrusted to you, so you will be governor of ten cities as your reward.'

¹⁸ "The next servant reported, 'Master, I invested your money and made five times the original amount.'

¹⁹ "'Well done!' the king said. 'You will be governor over five cities.'

²⁰ "But the third servant brought back only the original amount of money and said, 'Master, I hid your money and kept it safe. ²¹ I was afraid because you are a hard man to deal with, taking what isn't yours and harvesting crops you didn't plant.'

²² "'You wicked servant!' the king roared. 'Your own words condemn you. If you knew that I'm a hard man who takes what isn't mine and harvests crops I didn't plant, ²³ why didn't you deposit my money in the bank? At least I could have gotten some interest on it.'

²⁴ "Then, turning to the others standing nearby, the king ordered, 'Take the money from this servant, and give it to the one who has ten pounds.'

²⁵ "'But, master,' they said, 'he already has ten pounds!'

²⁶ "'Yes,' the king replied, 'and to those who use well what they are given, even more will be given. But from those who do nothing, even what little they have will be taken away. ²⁷ And as for these enemies of mine who didn't want me to be their king—bring them in and execute them right here in front of me.'"

5 MINUTES

Think about the following questions and how they might apply to your life.
- In this passage, the silver that was handed out to each servant represents different talents and abilities that God had given them. How would you define "talents and abilities"?
- What did the first two servants do with their silver (talents and abilities)? How did the king (God) respond? Why do you think he responded this way?

- Why do you think the king was so upset when the third servant hid his silver (talents and abilities) and did nothing with it?
- Just like the servants in this story, God has given you unique talents and abilities. What do you think they are? What are things that you really like to do and things you are really good at? If you are having a hard time thinking of some, ask a couple of people (like your mom, dad, best friends) what they think you do well.
- In what ways can you use your talents and abilities to honor God?

3 MINUTES

Hanging out with God

God has given everyone unique talents and abilities to be celebrated. God has given you special talents and abilities, and he has given them to each person in your family and each of your friends.

- In these 3 minutes, ask God to help you think about the talents and abilities of each family member and close friend. Grab a sheet of paper and write each of their names and what one or two things they do well.
- When you're finished, thank God for each person and for them being a part of your life. And if you want to do something really fun, tell each person what you came up with. EVERYBODY likes to be encouraged and told something that they're good at!

THOUGHTS

This space is here for you to jot down some thoughts, write out a prayer, draw a picture, or do whatever you want to help you remember your 10-minute moment.

THE MOST IMPORTANT COMMANDMENT

Day 24

When you prepare to take a test, don't you wish your teacher would identify the most important things you need to know? It'd be cool to look at the teacher and say, "You've talked about a lot of stuff here—can you just tell us what's MOST important, so we can just remember that?" Well, that's just what Jesus was asked in this section of The Red Stuff. Jesus was asked to identify the most important commandment, and Jesus picked two: Love God and love people.

Read the passage below. Circle or underline any words/phrases/verses that you feel are important to remember.

Mark 12:28-34 (NLT) (You can also read Luke's account in Luke 10:25-28 and Matthew's account in Matthew 22:34-40.)

28 One of the teachers of religious law was standing there listening to the debate. He realized that Jesus had answered well, so he asked, "Of all the commandments, which is the most important?"

29 Jesus replied, "The most important commandment is this: 'Listen, O Israel! The Lord our God is the one and only Lord. 30 And you must love the Lord your God with all your heart, all your soul, all your mind, and all your strength.' 31 The second is equally important: 'Love your neighbor as yourself.' No other commandment is greater than these."

32 The teacher of religious law replied, "Well said, Teacher. You have spoken the truth by saying that there is only one God and no other.

33 And I know it is important to love him with all my heart and all my understanding and all my strength, and to love my neighbor as myself. This is more important than to offer all of the burnt offerings and sacrifices required in the law."

34 Realizing how much the man understood, Jesus said to him, "You are not far from the Kingdom of God." And after that, no one dared to ask him any more questions."

5 MINUTES

Think about the following questions and how they might apply to your life.

- What's the most important commandment in verses 29-31?
- If you had to rate yourself on a scale from 1-10 (1 = not good; 10 = amazing), what number would you give yourself for loving God and loving others?
- In what four ways are we to love God (verse 30)? Why do you think Jesus included all of these?
- If one of the most important things we can do is love God, what are five ways you can show God that you love him?
- If loving other people is equally important to loving God, what are five ways you can show others that you love them?

3 MINUTES

Hanging out with God
- Mark 12:29-31 is the most important commandment in the Bible! One of the ways we can love God is knowing his Word. God tells us to keep his words close to our hearts so that we don't sin against him.

- Grab a piece of paper or an index card and write down the verses from today (Mark 12:28-34). Put it somewhere you will see every day. When you see it, read it out loud until you've memorized it. Don't forget to live it out, too!

This space is here for you to jot down some thoughts, write out a prayer, draw a picture, or do whatever you want to help you remember your 10-minute moment.

THE WIDOW'S OFFERING

Do you ever like to "people-watch"? You know, just look around and see what people are doing. You see some crazy things, huh? In this section of Red Stuff, Jesus was people-watching at the temple, near the place where people dropped off their offerings. From what we can tell, it seems like there were some rich people giving "impressive" amounts of money. And then a widow walks up with her offering and puts in "two small coins," probably worth less than a penny. But what does Jesus say? He claims that she gave more than the wealthy people who were putting in big amounts! How can that be?! Read on and see.

2 MINUTES

Read the passage below. Circle or underline any words/phrases/verses that you feel are important to remember.

Mark 12:41-44 (NLT) (You can also read Luke's account in Luke 21:1-4.)

41 Jesus sat down near the collection box in the Temple and watched as the crowds dropped in their money. Many rich people put in large amounts. 42 Then a poor widow came and dropped in two small coins.

43 Jesus called his disciples to him and said, "I tell you the truth, this poor widow has given more than all the others who are making contributions. 44 For they gave a tiny part of their surplus, but she, poor as she is, has given everything she had to live on."

5 MINUTES

Think about the following questions and how they might apply to your life.

- Verse 41 mentions a collection box or an offering basket at the temple. What is an offering?
- Why do you or people at your church give money as an offering?
- In verses 43 and 44, why did Jesus use the widow as an example and say that she gave more when it was clear that the rich people were giving larger amounts of money? Why does Jesus point out the widow's offering?
- So many of us live a "closed-fist" lifestyle; it's hard to share or give things away. Jesus turns things upside down and calls us to live an "open-hand" lifestyle, sharing with others and giving to those who are needy. Think about the possessions you have, or if you're in your own house, look at the stuff you own! Do you live with a "closed-fist" or an "open-hand" attitude?
- Is it difficult for you to live with an "open-hand" attitude? Why or why not? What might get in your way from living this kind of lifestyle?

3 MINUTES

Hanging out with God

- This will be an eye-opening exercise to do with God. Look around your room or your house for some of your most prized possessions and make a list.
- Spend the next several minutes with God. Share your list with him and what might be easy or tough for you to share or give away. When you talk to God about certain things that might be tough to share or give away, close your fist really tight to show that it's hard for you to let go of this item. Try to listen and see if God might want to tell you anything about this item, or about your "closed-fist" versus "open-hand" viewpoint. Slowly release your fist into an open hand to show that you are giving it to God.

TH●UGHTS

This space is here for you to jot down some thoughts, write out a prayer, draw a picture, or do whatever you want to help you remember your 10-minute moment.

HOW DO YOU GET TO GOD?

Maybe you've heard it said that "all religions are pretty much the same." Or that there are "many paths to get to God." Well, in this section of The Red Stuff, Jesus' words tell us something different. Jesus didn't just claim to be a righteous teacher, or a nice guy, or merely a sinless human. He said that he was actually the Son of God. And not only that, but that if you know Jesus, then you know God. That's a pretty remarkable claim! But Jesus didn't say this stuff to his followers so that they could tell everyone else how wrong they were. Jesus told people so they could know he loves them, and that he is the way to connect to the God who loves them, too!

2 MINUTES

Read the passage below. Circle or underline any words/phrases/verses that you feel are important to remember.

John 14:1-14 (NLT)
¹ *"Don't let your hearts be troubled. Trust in God, and trust also in me. ² There is more than enough room in my Father's home. If this were not so, would I have told you that I am going to prepare a place for you? ³ When everything is ready, I will come and get you, so that you will always be with me where I am. ⁴ And you know the way to where I am going."*

⁵ *"No, we don't know, Lord," Thomas said. "We have no idea where you are going, so how can we know the way?"*

⁶Jesus told him, "I am the way, the truth, and the life. No one can come to the Father except through me. ⁷If you had really known me, you would know who my Father is. From now on, you do know him and have seen him!"

⁸Philip said, "Lord, show us the Father, and we will be satisfied."

⁹Jesus replied, "Have I been with you all this time, Philip, and yet you still don't know who I am? Anyone who has seen me has seen the Father! So why are you asking me to show him to you? ¹⁰Don't you believe that I am in the Father and the Father is in me? The words I speak are not my own, but my Father who lives in me does his work through me. ¹¹Just believe that I am in the Father and the Father is in me. Or at least believe because of the work you have seen me do.

¹²"I tell you the truth, anyone who believes in me will do the same works I have done, and even greater works, because I am going to be with the Father. ¹³You can ask for anything in my name, and I will do it, so that the Son can bring glory to the Father. ¹⁴Yes, ask me for anything in my name, and I will do it!"

5 MINUTES

Think about the following questions and how they might apply to your life.

- Do you have friends who believe in a different religion than you or believe there are others paths that lead to God? If so, what do they believe?
- In verse 6, what does Jesus say is the only path that leads to God?
- Jesus also says that he is "the way, the truth, and the life." Describe what you think Jesus meant by "the way." What do you think he meant by "the truth"? And what about "the life"? Why do you think he picked these three specific words—why are they important?
- The disciples are having a tough time understanding what Jesus is trying to say. In verses 9-11, Jesus explains that if you have seen and know him, then you have seen and know God! Jesus is a reflection of God in human form! What things can you learn from Jesus about who God is?

3 MINUTES

Hanging out with God
- Did you know that there is so much to learn about God that you could wake up each morning for the rest of your life and learn something new about him? God is never boring and wants to be known by you!
- Spend the next couple of moments and ask God to show you something new about himself and see what happens! Try keeping a list, and then over time you can see all of the things you have learned about God.

THOUGHTS

This space is here for you to jot down some thoughts, write out a prayer, draw a picture, or do whatever you want to help you remember your 10-minute moment.

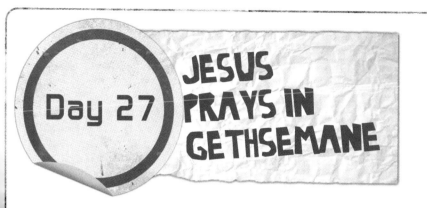

Day 27 — JESUS PRAYS IN GETHSEMANE

It's sometimes hard to remember that when Jesus lived on earth, even though he was the Son of God, he was still human, too. There were times he faced hard stuff in life that caused emotional pain. In this portion of Red Stuff, that's exactly what happens. Jesus tells his friends that his "soul is crushed with grief." So what does Jesus do in a moment like that? He stops everything he's doing and talks to God. He prays! And even though he doesn't get a magical answer in the first minute, he keeps talking to God. The place where he prayed is called "Gethsemane," sometimes identified as a garden. It was probably a group of trees, but the more important point is this: It was quiet, away from the busyness of life, and a great place to talk to God!

2 MINUTES

Read the passage below. Circle or underline any words/phrases/ verses that you feel are important to remember.

Matthew 26:36-46 (NLT) (You can also read Mark's account in Mark 14:32-42 and Luke's account in Luke 22:39-46.)

36 Then Jesus went with them to the olive grove called Gethsemane, and he said, "Sit here while I go over there to pray." 37 He took Peter and Zebedee's two sons, James and John, and he became anguished and distressed. 38 He told them, "My soul is crushed with grief to the point of death. Stay here and keep watch with me."

39 *He went on a little farther and bowed with his face to the ground, praying, "My Father! If it is possible, let this cup of suffering be taken away from me. Yet I want your will to be done, not mine."*

40 *Then he returned to the disciples and found them asleep. He said to Peter, "Couldn't you watch with me even one hour?* *41* *Keep watch and pray, so that you will not give in to temptation. For the spirit is willing, but the body is weak!"*

42 *Then Jesus left them a second time and prayed, "My Father! If this cup cannot be taken away unless I drink it, your will be done."* *43* *When he returned to them again, he found them sleeping, for they couldn't keep their eyes open.*

44 *So he went to pray a third time, saying the same things again.* *45* *Then he came to the disciples and said, "Go ahead and sleep. Have your rest. But look—the time has come. The Son of Man is betrayed into the hands of sinners.* *46* *Up, let's be going. Look, my betrayer is here!"*

Think about the following questions and how they might apply to your life.

- Jesus took some friends to go and pray at Gethsemane. Do you remember Zebedee's two sons, James and John, from an earlier passage we walked through? Look back to Day 22. What do you already know about these two brothers?
- Jesus had something heavy on his heart. What is the first thing he decided to do?
- How many times does it say that Jesus went off to pray? Why do you think he did this?
- It seems like Jesus' friends had no problem sleeping while Jesus spent time in prayer. Has something bothered you so much that you laid awake at night and could not sleep? If so, what was it? What did you do?
- Next time you are confronted with a heavy situation, what can you learn and apply from this Red Stuff?

3 MINUTES

Hanging out with God
- In this passage, Jesus was with some of his friends when he stopped to pray. Jesus needed some serious one-on-one time with God. If you were going to ask a couple of friends to pray with you, who would you invite and why?
- Find a trusted friend or an adult that you could pray with. Ask this person to pray for you and see what happens! If you can't think of anyone, ask God to help you find a friend like that.

THOUGHTS

This space is here for you to jot down some thoughts, write out a prayer, draw a picture, or do whatever you want to help you remember your 10-minute moment.

Is it ever "too late" to become a follower of Jesus? Some people ask if it's possible to have done so much wrong or to be so far from God, that you can't start a relationship with him. Of course it would seem like the church answer is that it's never too late. And these words in The Red Stuff agree with that! Two criminals were hanging on crosses right next to Jesus when he was executed. One of them stayed hard-hearted, even mocking Jesus in his last hours. But the other criminal recognized his own wrongdoing and admitted his sinfulness—and humbly asked Jesus if there was a place for him in heaven. Jesus' words show us that it's never too late!

Read the passage below. Circle or underline any words/phrases/ verses that you feel are important to remember.

Luke 23:32-43 (NLT)

32 Two others, both criminals, were led out to be executed with him. 33 When they came to a place called The Skull, they nailed him to the cross. And the criminals were also crucified—one on his right and one on his left.

34 Jesus said, "Father, forgive them, for they don't know what they are doing." And the soldiers gambled for his clothes by throwing dice.

35 The crowd watched and the leaders scoffed. "He saved others," they said, "let him save himself if he is really God's Messiah, the Chosen One." 36 The soldiers mocked him, too, by offering him a drink of sour wine. *37* They called out to him, "If you are the King of the Jews, save yourself!" *38* A sign was fastened to the cross above him with these words: "This is the King of the Jews."

39 One of the criminals hanging beside him scoffed, "So you're the Messiah, are you? Prove it by saving yourself—and us, too, while you're at it!"

40 But the other criminal protested, "Don't you fear God even when you have been sentenced to die? *41* We deserve to die for our crimes, but this man hasn't done anything wrong." *42* Then he said, "Jesus, remember me when you come into your Kingdom."

43 And Jesus replied, "I assure you, today you will be with me in paradise."

Think about the following questions and how they might apply to your life.
- Did you notice Jesus' attitude as he was being crucified on the cross? What were people saying and doing to him?
- Go back and read Luke 6:27-36 (from Day 6), then think about this passage. Does it surprise you how Jesus responded to those around him in Luke 23? Why or why not?
- What does Jesus pray in verse 34? How do you feel about this?
- One of the criminals continues to mock Jesus while the other admits his sins and asked for a place in heaven. How did Jesus respond to the second criminal in verse 43?
- Even in Jesus' toughest moment, he still chose to forgive others and have a relationship with them. How often do you stop to realize that you were once a sinner and Jesus did this for you?

Hanging out with God
- Sit and spend the next 3 minutes reading this passage again. Imagine being at The Skull where Jesus was crucified.

Imagine the noise of the crowd and Jesus hanging on the cross. He did this for you; he did this because he loves you and wants to save you so that you would have eternal life with him.

- Share with God what you are thinking and what you're feeling.

This space is here for you to jot down some thoughts, write out a prayer, draw a picture, or do whatever you want to help you remember your 10-minute moment.

Day 29

THOMAS DOUBTS

When it comes to faith, do you think "doubt" is a positive or negative trait? It sounds like a trick question, doesn't it? This section of Red Stuff happens after Jesus rose from the dead and appeared to the disciples. They saw him, alive, after they witnessed his death; they could hardly believe their eyes! But Thomas wasn't with them when it happened, so when his friends told him that they saw Jesus alive, he doubted it. When you read these words, look for Jesus' reaction. Was he upset or annoyed that Thomas was skeptical? It doesn't sound like it. But, read the last verse of this sentence carefully, as Jesus says something super important.

2 MINUTES

Read the passage below. Circle or underline any words/phrases/verses that you feel are important to remember.

John 20:19-29 (NLT)

19 That Sunday evening the disciples were meeting behind locked doors because they were afraid of the Jewish leaders. Suddenly, Jesus was standing there among them! "Peace be with you," he said. 20 As he spoke, he showed them the wounds in his hands and his side. They were filled with joy when they saw the Lord! 21 Again he said, "Peace be with you. As the Father has sent me, so I am sending you." 22 Then he breathed on them and said, "Receive the Holy Spirit. 23 If you forgive anyone's sins, they are forgiven. If you do not forgive them, they are not forgiven."

24 One of the twelve disciples, Thomas (nicknamed the Twin), was not with the others when Jesus came. 25 They told him, "We have seen the Lord!"

But he replied, "I won't believe it unless I see the nail wounds in his hands, put my fingers into them, and place my hand into the wound in his side."

²⁶ Eight days later the disciples were together again, and this time Thomas was with them. The doors were locked; but suddenly, as before, Jesus was standing among them. "Peace be with you," he said. ²⁷ Then he said to Thomas, "Put your finger here, and look at my hands. Put your hand into the wound in my side. Don't be faithless any longer. Believe!"

²⁸ "My Lord and my God!" Thomas exclaimed.

²⁹ Then Jesus told him, "You believe because you have seen me. Blessed are those who believe without seeing me."

Think about the following questions and how they might apply to your life.
- Imagine you were Thomas in this story. Do you think you would have reacted the same way when hearing the news from your friends that Jesus was alive? Why or why not?
- Do you think it's OK to doubt or have doubts about your faith? Why or why not?
- Have you ever had doubts about your faith? If so, what were they? Or what are they? Have you ever shared them with someone? If so, what happened?
- How did Jesus respond to Thomas? Based on Jesus' answer, what can we figure out about bringing our doubts to Jesus?
- In verse 29, Jesus says "Blessed are those who believe without seeing me." What do you think this means? Why is this so important?

Hanging out with God
- Sometimes it's scary to have doubts. But it's not the doubts that are actually scary (they're just thoughts); it's the fact that sometimes we feel that we're the only one with doubts.

- Hang out with God today and share some of your doubts with him. Maybe you have doubts about your relationship with God, maybe it's about something in your life, or maybe it's about yourself. Whatever it is, remember how Jesus approached Thomas—and that God is big enough to handle our doubts!

THOUGHTS

This space is here for you to jot down some thoughts, write out a prayer, draw a picture, or do whatever you want to help you remember your 10-minute moment.

Day 30
THE GREAT COMMISSION

"The Great Commission" is a famous phrase from the Bible, but do you know what it means? A "commission" is what you do when you give someone an important direction—or send someone on a mission. The Great Commission is The Red Stuff that Jesus spoke to his followers after he came back to life. Jesus wanted to be clear about what the church should be about! If we're not careful, the church can become like a Christian club or a holy huddle of people hiding from all the bad stuff in the world. But that's never what Jesus intended for the church! There were a few things that Jesus was specific about as he clarified the mission of the church for those first disciples and for us. Look for them as you read this passage.

Read the passage below. Circle or underline any words/phrases/ verses that you feel are important to remember.

Matthew 28:16-20 (NLT) (You can also read Mark's account in Mark 16:15-20.)

16 Then the eleven disciples left for Galilee, going to the mountain where Jesus had told them to go. 17 When they saw him, they worshiped him—but some of them doubted!

18 Jesus came and told his disciples, "I have been given all authority in heaven and on earth. 19 Therefore, go and make disciples of all the nations, baptizing them in the name of the Father and the Son and the Holy Spirit. 20 Teach these new disciples to obey all the commands I have given you. And be sure of this: I am with you always, even to the end of the age."

Think about the following questions and how they might apply to your life.
- What is Jesus' Great Commission in verses 19 and 20?
- What do you think it means to "make disciples"?
- As you look at your church and your friends at church, how well are you fulfilling this commission?
- In what ways are you living out the Great Commission, and what are some areas you could grow in?
- Jesus finished this passage saying, "And be sure of this: I am with you always, even to the end of the age." Why do you think Jesus said this or reminded us of this after sharing the Great Commission?

Hanging out with God
- This passage is one of the last conversations recorded of Jesus with his disciples. People say that someone's last words can be the most memorable words that person ever says.
- In these next 3 minutes, share with God some of the most powerful passages and words of Jesus that you have read so far. Why were they so powerful to you?
- Spend time thanking God for Jesus and what you have learned.

THOUGHTS

This space is here for you to jot down some thoughts, write out a prayer, draw a picture, or do whatever you want to help you remember your 10-minute moment.

Day 31

GOOD FRUIT

Did you ever hear someone brag about their skills, but you wonder if they're able to back up their words? Like maybe they're just bragging because there's no evidence to prove them wrong. (My dad always used to say, "Talk is cheap." I think this is what he meant!) It can be hard to know if we can trust someone's words, even when they're making claims about their loyalty to God and living his way. But Jesus tells us in The Red Stuff how we can check out someone's claim about themselves. Not only that, but looking at your own "fruit" is a way to check out whether you're living the way God wants you to!

Read the passage below. Circle or underline any words/phrases/ verses that you feel are important to remember.

Luke 6:43-45 (NLT) (You can also read Matthew's account in Matthew 7:15-20.)

43 "A good tree can't produce bad fruit, and a bad tree can't produce good fruit. 44 A tree is identified by its fruit. Figs are never gathered from thornbushes, and grapes are not picked from bramble bushes. 45 A good person produces good things from the treasury of a good heart, and an evil person produces evil things from the treasury of an evil heart. What you say flows from what is in your heart."

5 MINUTES

Think about the following questions and how they might apply to your life.

- In this passage, the tree represents a person (like you and me) and the fruit represents the way a person acts. In your own words, explain what Jesus means in Luke 6:43-44 when he talks about good and bad trees and good and bad fruit.
- Describe a person who bears good fruit in life. Describe a person who bears bad fruit in life. Can you think of people you know that fit each example?
- Grab your Bible and read Matthew 7:15-20. This is Matthew's account of Jesus talking about good fruit. What are the similarities in these passages, and what's unique?
- If your parents were asked to judge you by your fruit (actions), what do you think they would say? If your friends were asked to judge you by your fruit (actions), what do you think they would say? Would the answers that your parents and friends give be similar or different? If different, why do you think that is?
- At the end of Luke 6:45, what does Jesus say will indicate whether someone has a good or evil heart? How important do you think this is?

3 MINUTES

Hanging out with God

- We can connect with God in many ways! Think about how you'd like to hang out with God today. Go with your gut reaction—whether it's going to the park, staying in your room, or shooting hoops with him, let God know what's going on in your life. This includes events of the day, how you're feeling, any thoughts or concerns you might have—anything! And think about asking God to help you reflect on your "good fruit" based on the above verses, and if there's any way he wants you to respond.

THOUGHTS

This space is here for you to jot down some thoughts, write out
a prayer, draw a picture, or do whatever you want to help you
remember your 10-minute moment.

Congratulations! WOOHOO!

You have succeeded in reading a whole bunch of The Red Stuff—and putting God's Word in your heart! And if you've taken the time to answer the questions and hang with God after reading his Word, I'm betting that you've noticed a difference in your friendship with him. How cool is that?! Psalm 119 is a cool description of the power that God's Word has—check out verse 105: "Your word is a lamp to guide my feet and a light for my path." Having The Red Stuff in your head is like having a flashlight in your hands on a night when the electricity is out!

So…what's next? Well, I'd say DON'T STOP NOW! Keep the momentum going in your relationship with God. You could pick up another 10 Minute Moments book (yep, there are more of 'em) or another Bible study to keep you reading and thinking about God's genius wisdom. Glance back over this book, and look at your notes or journal to see what God might be encouraging you to do next. He has loads of wisdom for whatever you're wondering about!

It's been fun sharing The Red Stuff with you!

Scott

Scott Rubin